AMERICAN PRESIDENTS

THOMAS JEFFERSON

Cataloging-in-Publication Data

Names: James, India.
Title: Thomas Jefferson / India James.
Description: Buffalo, NY : Norwood House Press, 2027. | Series: American presidents | Includes glossary and index.
Identifiers: ISBN 9781978579996 (pbk.) | ISBN 9781978580008 (library bound) | ISBN 9781978580015 (ebook)
Subjects: LCSH: Jefferson, Thomas, 1743-1826--Juvenile literature. | Presidents--United States--Biography--Juvenile literature. | Legislators--United States--Biography--Juvenile literature.
Classification: LCC E332. J36 2027 | DDC 973.46092--dc23

Published in 2027 by
Norwood House Press
2544 Clinton Street
Buffalo, NY 14224

Designer: Rhea Magaro
Editor: Kim Thompson

Photo credits: Cover, p. 1 The White House; p. 5 OJUP/Shutterstock.com; p. 6 Thomas Soellner/Shutterstock.com; pp. 7, 9-12, 15-16, 20 Library of Congress; p. 8 Paul R. Kucher IV; p. 13 Stuart, Gilbert; p. 19 BrianPIrwin/Shutterstock.com; p. 21 Sean Pavone/Shutterstock.com;

Printed in the United States of America

CPSIA compliance information: Batch #CSNHP27: For further information contact Norwood House Press at 1-800-237-9932.

TABLE OF CONTENTS

Early Years

Thomas Jefferson was born on April 13, 1743, in Shadwell, Virginia. He lived on a **plantation** with his parents and nine brothers and sisters. He loved to explore the woods, read, and study.

Birthplace in Virginia

When Thomas was nine, he left home to live at school. He studied subjects like science, math, French, and dancing.

In 1760, Thomas went to the College of William and Mary in Virginia. He took classes to become a **lawyer**.

Building a Career

Thomas worked as a lawyer. He married Martha Wayles Skelton in 1772. The couple had six children. They lived near Charlottesville, Virginia, in a house that Thomas designed. It was on a plantation called Monticello.

America was not yet a country. Virginia was a **colony** of Great Britain. Thomas did not like how American colonists were treated. They paid taxes, but they had no say in the British government. Many others felt the same way.

A group of men formed the **Continental Congress**. They represented the 13 colonies. In 1776, they asked Thomas to write the Declaration of Independence.

IN CONGRESS, JULY 4, 1776.

The unanimous Declaration of the thirteen united States of America,

The document declared that America was no longer under British rule. It said, "We hold these truths to be self-evident, that all men are created equal, that they are endowed by their Creator with certain **unalienable** Rights, that among these are Life, Liberty and the pursuit of Happiness."

The United States won the Revolutionary War against Great Britain. It was a free nation. Thomas served his new country. He was the governor of Virginia. He was the nation's **secretary of state**.

John Adams was the second U.S. president. Thomas Jefferson was his vice president.

Presidency

Thomas Jefferson was elected the third president of the United States in 1800. He got the same number of votes as his opponent. Congress decided that Thomas should win. He served as president for two **terms**.

The Louisiana Purchase

President Jefferson is famous for making the Louisiana Purchase. At the time, France owned most of the land west of the Mississippi River. Thomas helped America buy it from France. It nearly doubled the size of the country.

Later Life

After leaving the White House, Thomas moved back to Monticello. Education had always been important to him. He helped start the University of Virginia. Today, it is one of the country's leading **institutions** of higher learning.

Thomas died on July 4, 1826. The day was exactly 50 years after the signing of the Declaration of Independence.

Thomas Jefferson is remembered as a founding father of the United States of America.

Glossary

colony (KAH-luh-nee): a territory settled by people from another country and controlled by that country; American colonists came from Europe to live and work in colonies governed by Great Britain

Continental Congress (KAHN-tuh-nen-tuhl KANG-gris): a group of delegates that served as the government of the 13 original colonies from 1774 to 1789

institutions (in-sti-TOO-shuhnz): large organizations where people work or live together

lawyer (LAW-yur): a person whose job is to represent people in a court of law and to give advice about the law

plantation (plan-TAY-shuhn): a large farm in a warm climate; workers on many American plantations, including Monticello, were enslaved Black people—Thomas Jefferson and many other early American leaders were enslavers

secretary of state (SEK-ri-ter-ee ov state): a person in the U.S. government who is responsible for making agreements with other countries

terms (turmz): definite or set periods of time; American presidents are elected to terms that last four years

unalienable (uhn-AY-lee-uhn-uh-buhl): impossible to take away or give up

Thinking Questions

1. What did Thomas study in school?
2. What important document did Thomas write?
3. How did Thomas double the size of the country?
4. What university was founded by Thomas Jefferson?
5. Why do you think Thomas Jefferson is called a founding father of the United States?

Index

About the Author

India James writes about science, technology, math, and history for young readers. She loves learning new things while writing books. India lives in Ohio with her family.